Wildflower Wreath

PLATE 1

Test Pattern

PLATE 2

Blue Flag

Test Pattern

Buttercup

PLATE 3

PLATE 4   Violet

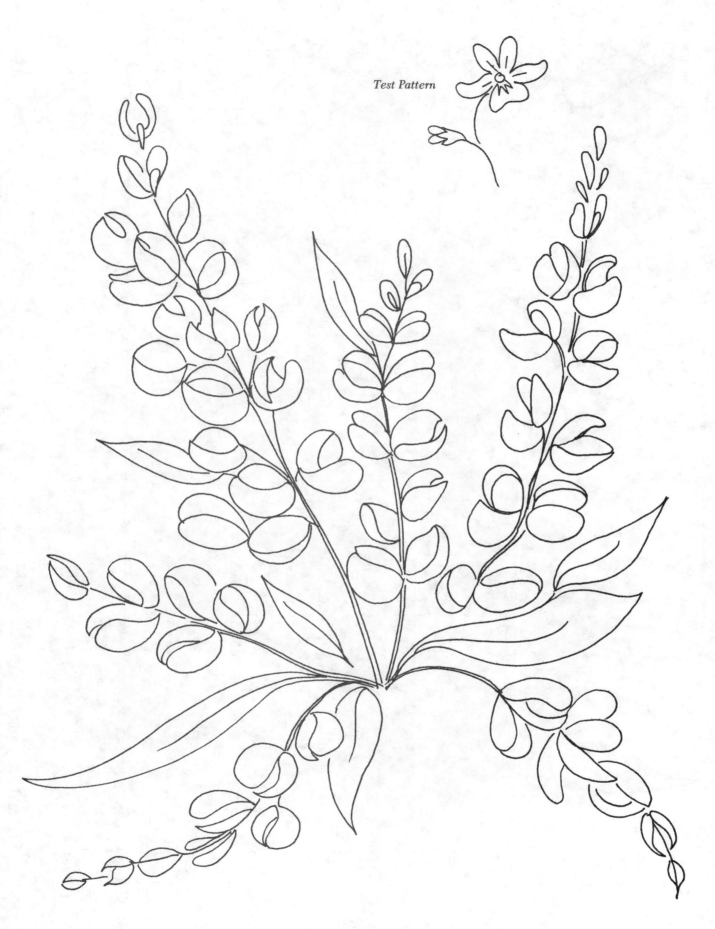

Test Pattern

Texas Bluebonnet

PLATE 5

Texas Bluebonnet

Test Pattern

PLATE 6

Periwinkle

Cornflower

PLATE 7

Cornflower

Test Pattern

PLATE 8

Daisy

Test Pattern

Hepatica or Liverwort

PLATE 9

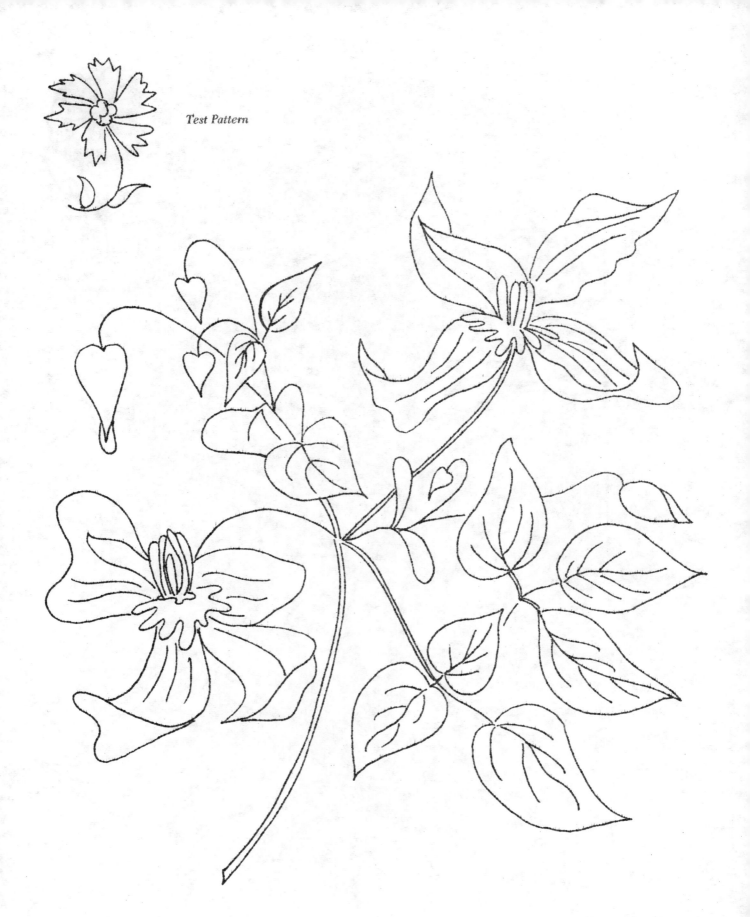

Test Pattern

PLATE 10

Clematis

Test Pattern

Gentian

PLATE 11

PLATE 23

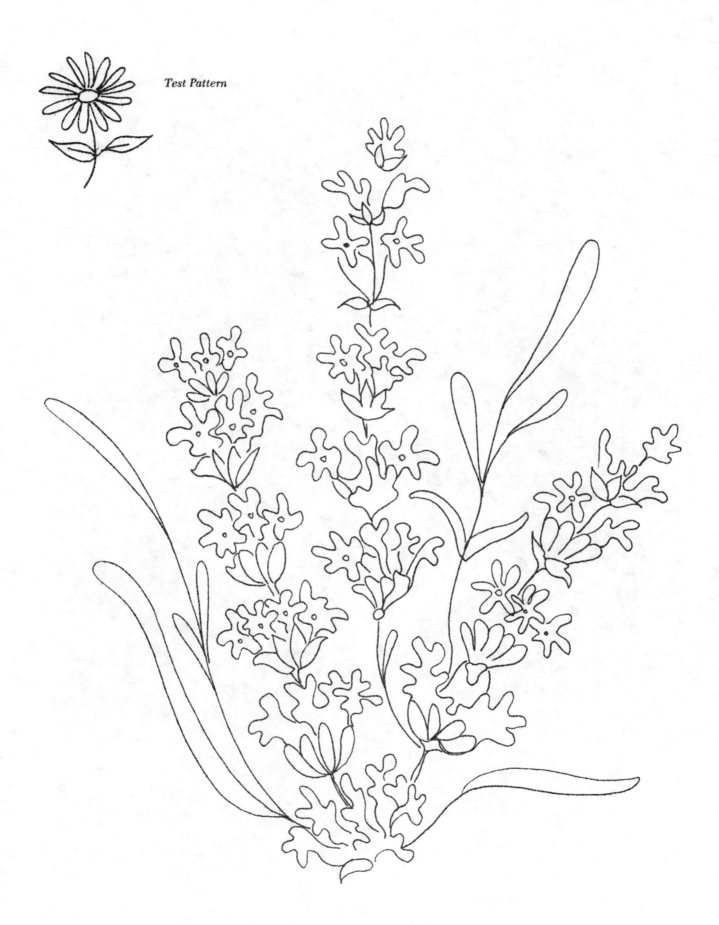

Test Pattern

PLATE 12

Sea Lavender

Wild Rose, Violet, Buttercup
and Forget-me-not

Cornflower, Harebell
and Forget-me-not

PLATE 13

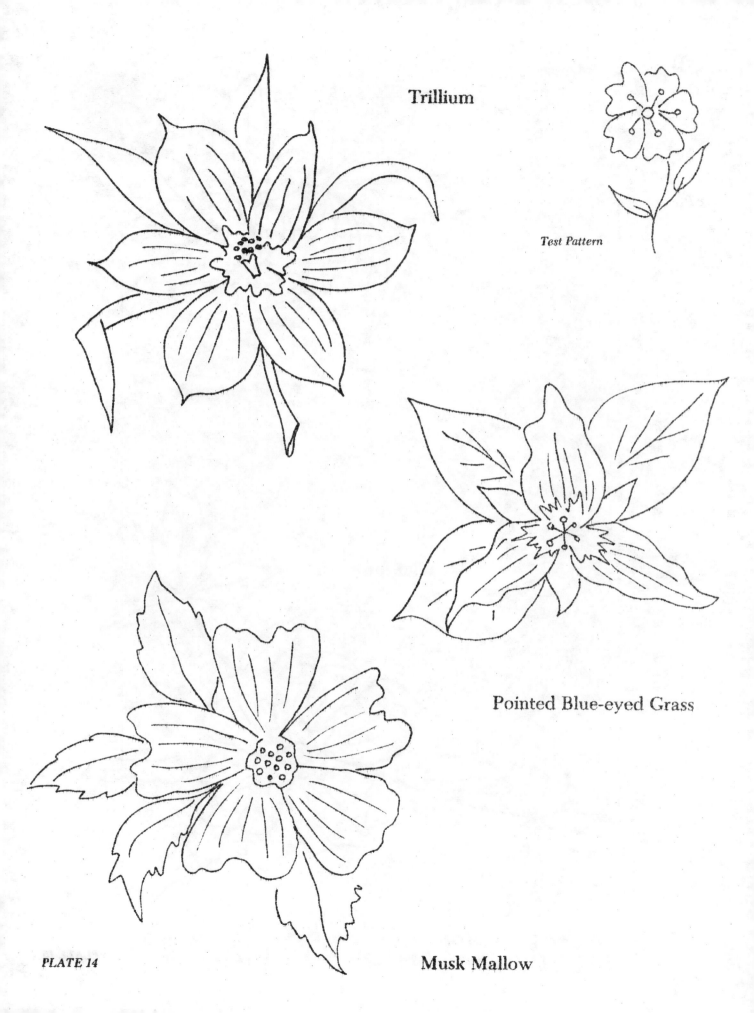

Trillium

Test Pattern

Pointed Blue-eyed Grass

PLATE 14

Musk Mallow

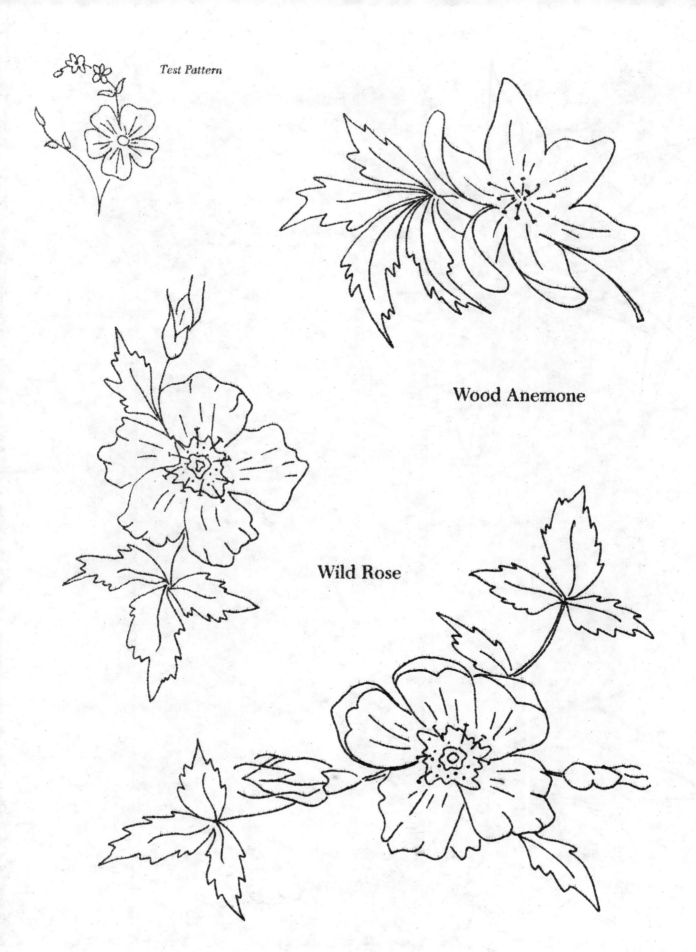

Test Pattern

Wood Anemone

Wild Rose

PLATE 15

Wood Anemone

Wild Rose

PLATE 16

All-Blue Borders:
Forget-me-not,
Virginia Bluebell and
New England Aster

PLATE 16.

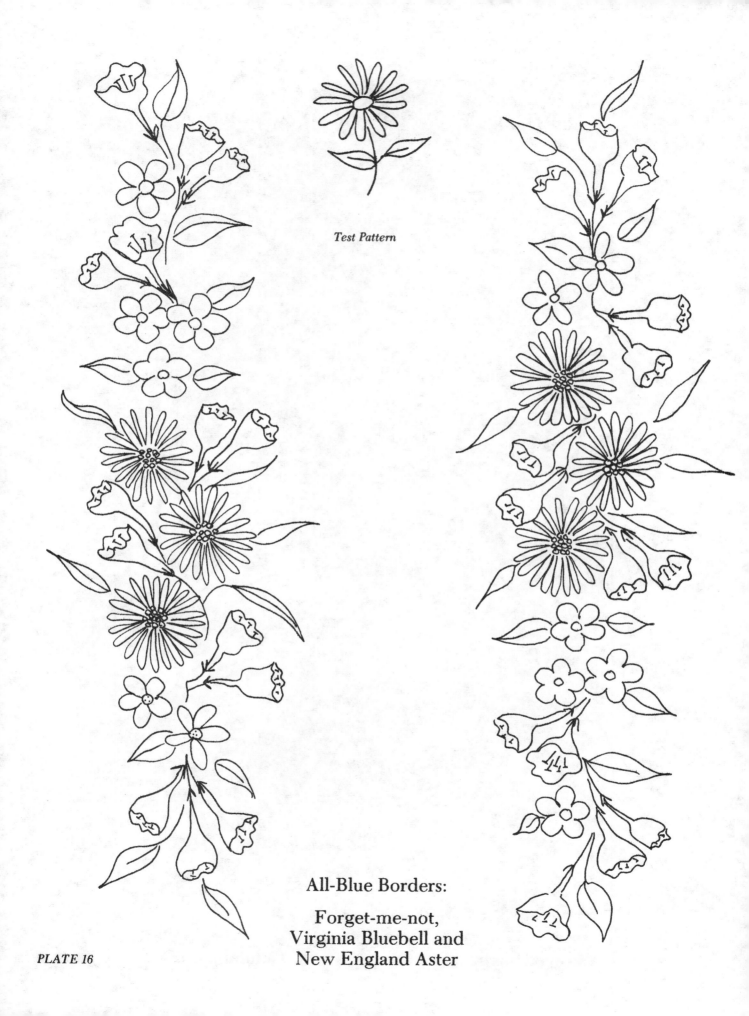

Test Pattern

All-Blue Borders:

Forget-me-not,
Virginia Bluebell and
New England Aster

PLATE 16

Test Pattern

Black-eyed Susan   Columbine   *PLATE 17*

Thistle

Wild Geranium

Wild Flax

Trailing Arbutus

PLATE 35

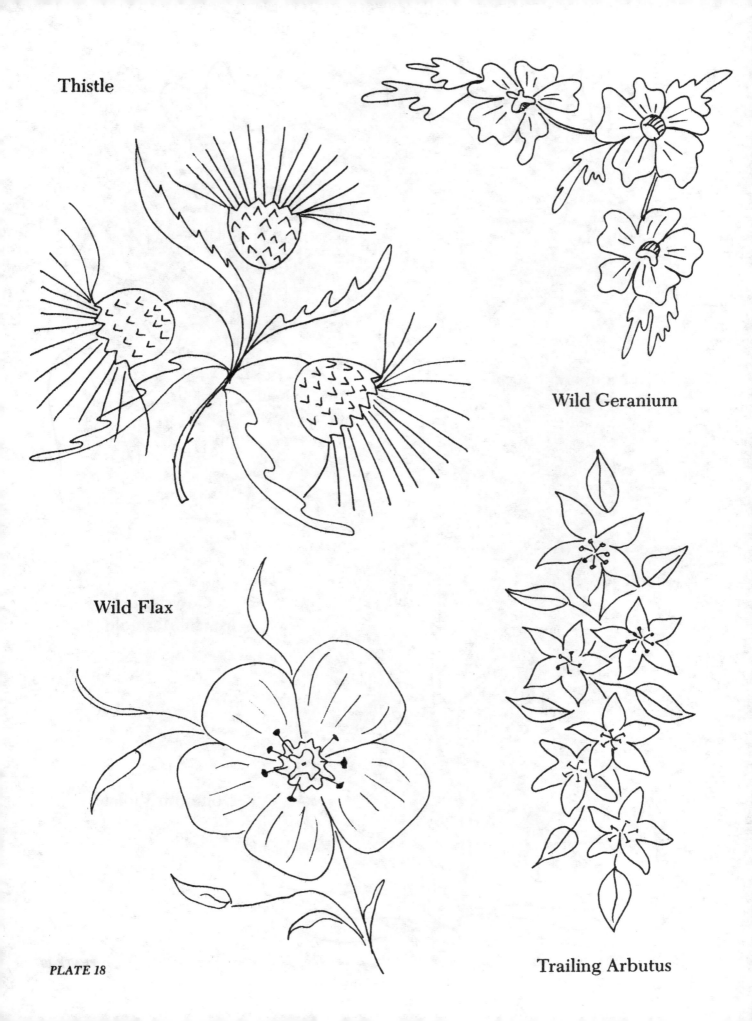

Thistle

Wild Geranium

Wild Flax

PLATE 18

Trailing Arbutus

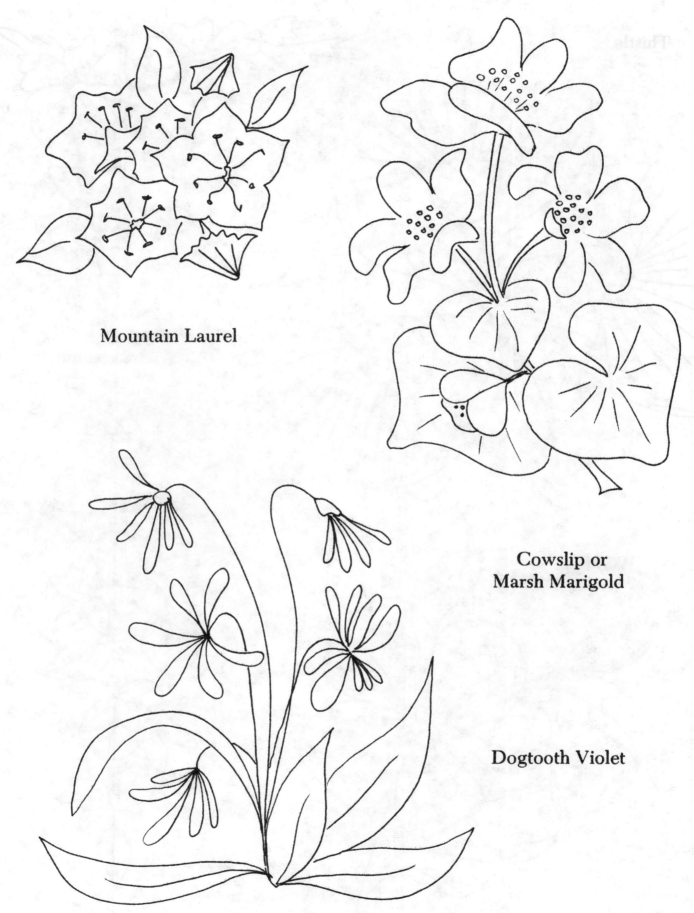

Mountain Laurel

Cowslip or
Marsh Marigold

Dogtooth Violet

PLATE 19

Mountain Laurel

Cowslip or
Marsh Marigold

Dogtooth Violet

PLATE 19

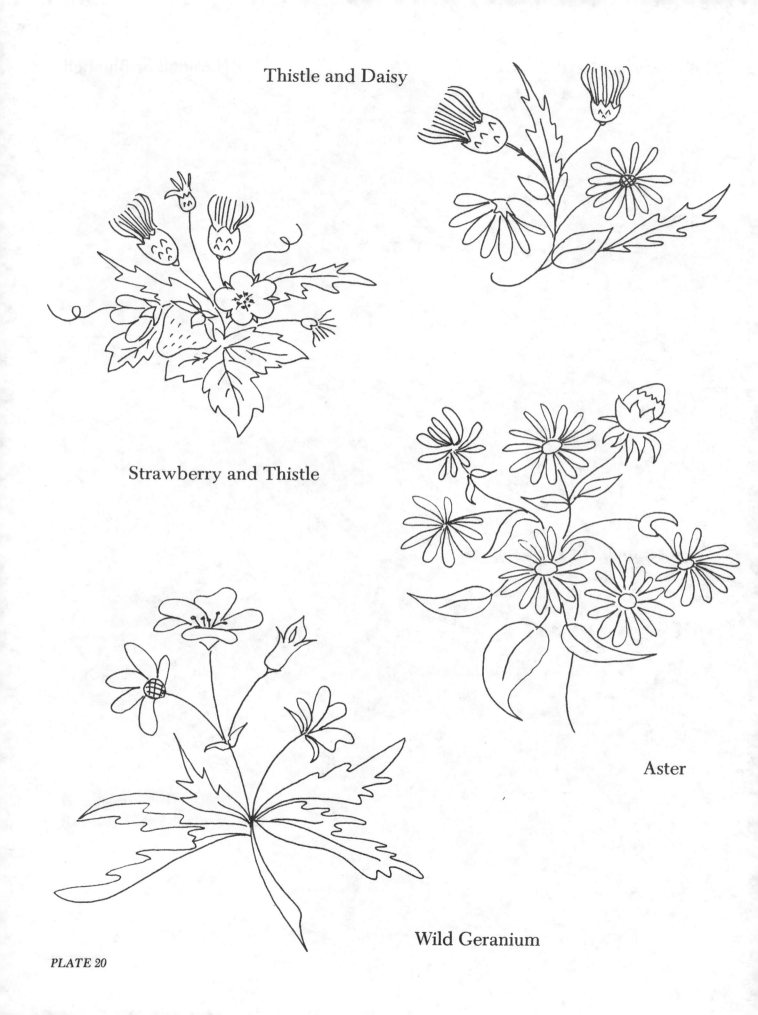

Thistle and Daisy

Strawberry and Thistle

Aster

Wild Geranium

PLATE 20

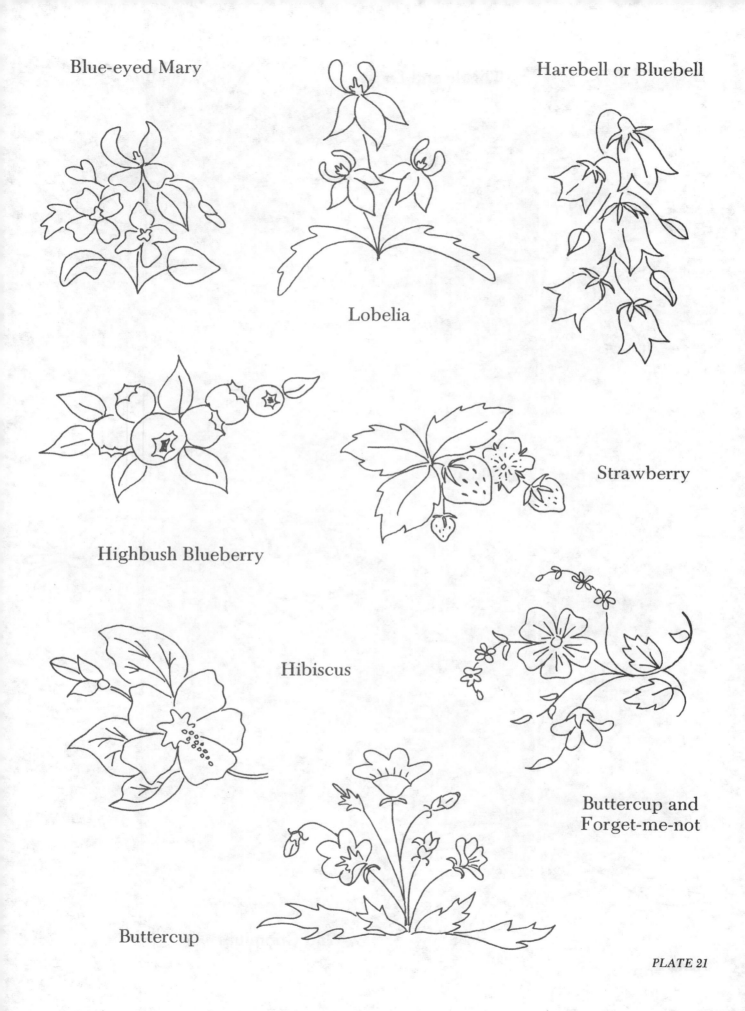

Blue-eyed Mary

Lobelia

Harebell or Bluebell

Highbush Blueberry

Strawberry

Hibiscus

Buttercup and
Forget-me-not

Buttercup

PLATE 21

Bog Rosemary

Harebell or Bluebell

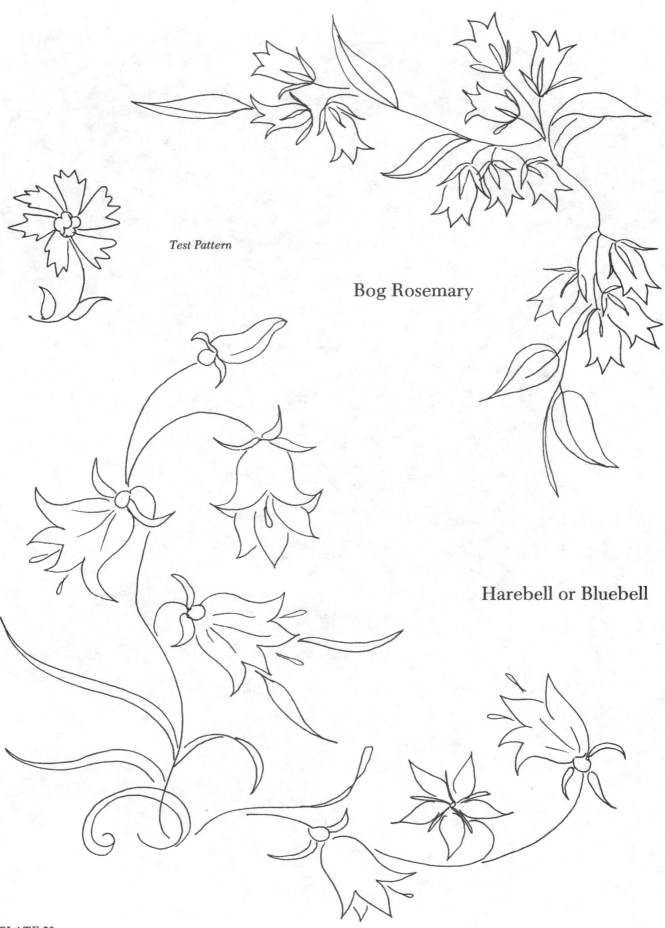

Test Pattern

Bog Rosemary

Harebell or Bluebell

PLATE 22

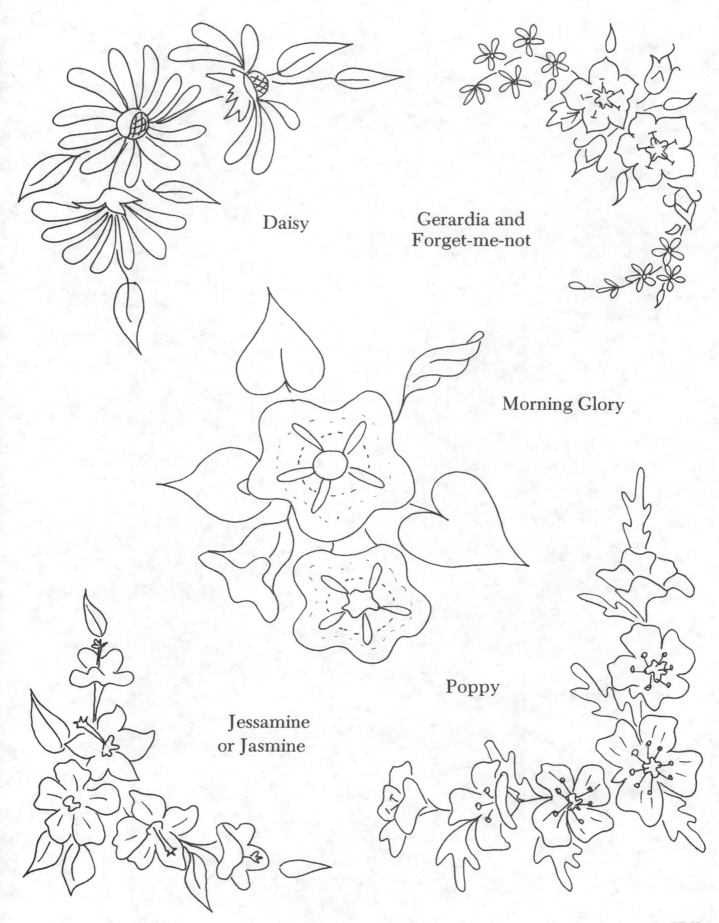

Daisy

Gerardia and
Forget-me-not

Morning Glory

Poppy

Jessamine
or Jasmine

PLATE 23

PLATE 34

Test Pattern

PLATE 24   Wildflower Bouquet